DOG BREEDS

Golden Retrievers

by Mari Schuh

Consultant:
Michael Leuthner, D.V.M.
PetCare Clinic, Madison, Wisc.

BELLWETHER MEDIA • MINNEAPOLIS, MN

Note to Librarians, Teachers, and Parents:

Blastoff! Readers are carefully developed by literacy experts and combine standards-based content with developmentally appropriate text.

Level 1 provides the most support through repetition of high-frequency words, light text, predictable sentence patterns, and strong visual support.

Level 2 offers early readers a bit more challenge through varied simple sentences, increased text load, and less repetition of high-frequency words.

Level 3 advances early-fluent readers toward fluency through increased text and concept load, less reliance on visuals, longer sentences, and more literary language.

Level 4 builds reading stamina by providing more text per page, increased use of punctuation, greater variation in sentence patterns, and increasingly challenging vocabulary.

Level 5 encourages children to move from "learning to read" to "reading to learn" by providing even more text, varied writing styles, and less familiar topics.

Whichever book is right for your reader, Blastoff! Readers are the perfect books to build confidence and encourage a love of reading that will last a lifetime!

This edition first published in 2009 by Bellwether Media.

No part of this publication may be reproduced in whole or in part without written permission of the publisher. For information regarding permission, write to Bellwether Media Inc., Attention: Permissions Department, Post Office Box 19349, Minneapolis, MN 55419-0349.

Library of Congress Cataloging-in-Publication Data
Schuh, Mari C., 1975-
   Golden retrievers / by Mari Schuh.
      p. cm. — (Blastoff! readers. Dog breeds)
   Includes bibliographical references and index.
   Summary: "Simple text and full color photographs introduce beginning readers to the characteristics of the dog breed Golden Retrievers . Developed by literacy experts for students in kindergarten through third grade"—Provided by publisher.
   ISBN-13: 978-1-60014-216-1 (hardcover : alk. paper)
   ISBN-10: 1-60014-216-8 (hardcover : alk. paper)
   1. Golden retriever—Juvenile literature. I. Title.

SF429.G63S39 2008
636.752'7—dc22
                                                            2008020002

Contents

What Are Golden Retrievers?

With their friendly nature and endless energy, the Golden Retriever **breed** is a very popular dog. They are most often kept as hunting dogs and family pets.

The first Golden Retrievers helped people hunt ducks and other wild birds. They are excellent **water retrievers**. When hunters shoot wild birds, the birds often fall into swamps or lakes. Water retrievers swim out to find the birds and bring them back to the hunter.

The **coat** of a Golden Retriever can be any shade of golden brown. As they get older, they may get gray or white hair on their face or body. They have thick hair that grows long on their neck, legs, and tail. Their coats can be straight or wavy.

! fun fact

Golden Retrievers do not make good watchdogs. They are too friendly!

Golden Retrievers have short ears, a broad head, a strong neck, and a long, straight tail. They weigh around 65 pounds (29.5 kilograms) and stand 23 to 24 inches (58.4 to 61 centimeters) high at the shoulders.

History of Golden Retrievers

The Golden Retriever breed began in Scotland. This country is part of Great Britain. A man named Lord Tweedmouth had a Yellow Retriever named Nous. Dogs of this breed could retrieve birds on land but were not good swimmers.

Lord Tweedmouth wanted a new dog that could retrieve and liked to swim. He knew that Tweed Water Spaniels were good swimmers. Nous and a Tweed Water Spaniel had four yellow puppies.

Lord Tweedmouth also chose other dogs to have puppies. He found more dogs that could swim well. He also chose dogs with thick golden coats. He knew a thick coat would keep dogs warm in cold water. The result of all of this was the Golden Retriever.

! fun fact

Former United States President Gerald Ford owned a Golden Retriever named Liberty. Liberty grew up at the White House. She also had her first litter of puppies at the White House.

Golden Retrievers are the hunting dogs that Lord Tweedmouth wanted. They are powerful swimmers and can retrieve prey from land or water.

Golden Retrievers first came to the United States in the 1890s. They soon became popular hunting dogs and pets.

Golden Retrievers Today

Golden Retrievers are intelligent and easy to train. Their ability to obey commands makes them good at doing many kinds of work.

Golden Retrievers are often used as **working dogs**. Some Golden Retrievers work as guide dogs for people who are blind.

Other Golden Retrievers can pull wheelchairs and push elevator buttons. They can carry supplies for people in a special coat with lots of pockets.

Some Golden Retrievers visit people who are in the hospital. The friendly dogs help cheer people up.

Golden Retrievers can also use their great sense of smell to help people. They help police by sniffing for illegal drugs. They can also lead rescue teams to people who are lost.

Golden Retrievers are active, sweet, and **athletic** dogs. They need lots of exercise to stay happy and healthy. When happy, Golden Retrievers can be hard workers and playful pets.

Glossary

athletic—good at activities that use strength, speed, and skill

breed—a type of dog

coat—the hair or fur of an animal

water retriever—a dog that gets something and brings it back from the water; water retrievers fetch prey such as wild ducks from rivers, marshes, and swamps.

working dog—a breed of dog that does jobs to help people

To Learn More

AT THE LIBRARY

Gray, Susan H. *Golden Retrievers*. Chanhassen, Minn.: Child's World, 2007.

Murray, Julie. *Golden Retrievers*. Edina, Minn.: Buddy Books, 2004.

Trumbauer, Lisa. *Golden Retrievers*. Mankato, Minn.: Pebble Books, 2006.

ON THE WEB

Learning more about Golden Retrievers is as easy as 1, 2, 3.

1. Go to www.factsurfer.com

2. Enter "Golden Retrievers" into search box.

3. Click the "Surf" button and you will see a list of related web sites.

With factsurfer.com, finding more information is just a click away.

Index

The images in this book are reproduced through the courtesy of: Varina and Jay Patel, front cover; Pix 'n Pages, pp. 4, 5, 6, 10-11, 14-15, 20; Mark Raycroft / Getty Images, pp. 7, 17, 21; imagebroker / Alamy, pp. 8-9; Mike Brinson / Getty Images, p. 12; ARCO/C. Steimer / age fotostock, p. 13; Boris Djuranovic, p. 16; iofoto, p. 18; Mark Rose, p.19.